The best hats

Story by Annette Smith   Illustrations by Susy Boyer Rigby

The children made some hats.

"I like your hat, Meg," said Ben.
"It looks like a bird!"

The teacher said,
"I like all of your hats.
They look **beautiful**."

"Can we have a hat day at school?"
said the children.

"Yes," said the teacher.
"Your mothers and fathers
can come and see your hats
on Friday.
They can have hats on, too."

6

"My mom and dad
can't come to school,"
said Meg.
"They go to work."

"But your grandma can come,"
said the teacher.

On Friday,

Hannah's dad came to school.

He had his fishing hat on.

Ben's mom had her sunhat on.

Meg looked out the window.

"I can't see my grandma," she said.

"She will come, Meg,"
said the teacher.

"Your grandma will not forget."

12

"Meg! Here comes your grandma," shouted Ben.

"But she has not got a hat."

"She has a big box," said Meg.

Meg's grandma opened the box, and the children looked inside.

14

Grandma said, "I made a hat, too."

"Your hat looks like
a bird's nest, Grandma," said Meg.
"I can see some eggs in it."

Grandma laughed.
"It's a nest for your bird," she said.

"We have the best hats of all,"
laughed Meg.